If Whitman were born in the Midwest to Mennonite parents, listened to Dylan and the Dead and loved to laugh at himself, he'd sound just like Jeff Gundy. "I want the reader as far inside of my skin as possible," he writes, in bemused poems that are in love with the productions of matter and time. "How else to describe this absurd, lovely world?" he poses in the title poem of his warm and inviting *Abandoned Homeland*. Gundy's poetry reminds us, over and over, that paying attention to the delights and troubles of existence becomes a kind of psalm to this botched and beautiful creation.
—Philip Metres, author of *Sand Opera*

Other Books by Jeff Gundy

Poetry:

Somewhere Near Defiance. Anhinga, 2014.
Spoken among the Trees. Univ. of Akron Press, 2007.
Deerflies. WordTech Editions, 2004.
Rhapsody with Dark Matter. Bottom Dog Press, 2000.
Flatlands. Cleveland State Univ. Poetry Center, 1995.
Inquiries. Bottom Dog Press, 1992.

Poetry Chapbooks:

Greatest Hits 1986-2003. Pudding House Publications, 2003.
Surrendering to the Real Things. Pikestaff Press, 1986.
Johnny America Takes on Mother Nature. Pinchpenny Press, 1975.
Back Home in Babylon. Pinchpenny Press, 1974.

Essays/Creative Nonfiction:

Songs from an Empty Cage: Poetry, Mystery, Anabaptism, and Peace. Cascadia Press, 2013.
Walker in the Fog: On Mennonite Writing. Cascadia Press, 2005.
Scattering Point: The World in a Mennonite Eye. SUNY Press, 2003.
A Community of Memory: My Days with George and Clara. Univ. of Illinois Press, 1996.

ABANDONED HOMELAND

POEMS BY
JEFF GUNDY

HARMONY SERIES
BOTTOM DOG PRESS
HURON, OHIO

General Editor: Larry Smith
Cover Design: Susanna Sharp-Schwacke
Cover Image: Michael Creese

ACKNOWLEDGMENTS

Many thanks to the editors of the journals where these poems first appeared, some in different versions:
About Place: "Kelleys Island Elegy with Wind and Hearsay," "Things I Didn't Learn from the Road"; *Adirondack Review:* "We Write with Our Bodies," "First Notes on Border Crossings"; *Brevity:* "Safety"; *Cape Rock:* "Map of My Self," "The Unreliable Narrator Reports on the Narrative Workshop," "Meditation with Gravel and Quilt"; *Center for Mennonite Writing Journal (online):* "Fifty Billion Planets," "Three for Trakl"; *Cincinnati Review:* "Partial Catalog, April Sunday"; *Christian Century:* "Natural Theology from the Sherman Bench," "Free Will in the Late Capitalist Era"; *The Cresset:* "Meditation on Matter"; *Hamilton Stone Review:* "Prints," "That the Grotesque Inhabits the Material World," "On Explanation: Quasi-Ghazal"; *Image:* "Further Notes on the Martyrs," "Being the Song"; *Kenyon Review Online:* "Meditation on Narrative, Dogma, and Flight"; *Kestrel:* "Ambitions," "Cookies"; *Moon City Review:* "Waterfall"; *Nimrod:* "Subjunctive on Burntside Lake," "Contemplation with Doors, Nests, and Music," "The Body"; *North American Review:* "Brief History of Midwestern Civilization"; *Poetry East:* "Pavilion"; *Poetry Salzburg Review:* "Reading Neil Gaiman in a Western Suburb," "Why I Get Through Most Days in Prose," "March Ode on Beauty and Melancholy (Three Drafts)"; *Rhubarb:* "The Eight Sounds," "Contemplation with Old Honda, Carnality, Fish," "In Boston," "Summer Early in the Millennium"; *Rock and Sling:* "Contemplation with Acorns and Guitar," "Improvisations among the Ledges," "From the Province of Heron and Swallowtail," "Listening for Orpheus," "The Sorrow Induced by an Inexact Vocabulary"; *Saint Katherine Review:* "Something Is"; *Seminary Ridge Review:* "Inventory and Interiority at Merry Lea"; *Shenandoah:* "Thread"; *Stardust Gazette:* "What Do We Mean"; *Your Impossible Voice:* "Meditation with Good Posture and Swine Flu"

"Brief History of Midwestern Civilization" was a finalist for *North American Review's* 2014 James Hearst Poetry Prize.

Acknowledgments Continued on page 87.

TABLE OF CONTENTS

I.

THE BODY 9
WHAT DO WE MEAN 11
INVENTORY AND INTERIORITY AT MERRY LEA 12
SUMMER EARLY IN THE MILLENNIUM 13
CONTEMPLATION WITH OLD HONDA, CARNALITY, FISH 14
READING NEIL GAIMAN IN A WESTERN SUBURB 16
CONTEMPLATION WITH DOORS, NESTS, AND MUSIC 17
THINGS I DIDN'T LEARN FROM THE ROAD 19
THREAD 20
THE POET WATCHES HIS NEIGHBORHOOD 21
APRIL WITH GARDEN AND GUILT 23
WHY I GET THROUGH MOST DAYS IN PROSE 24
SAFETY 25
PRINTS 26
ODE WITH WINTER SUNSHINE, ONE MIND, FOUR HOUSES 27
CONTEMPLATION WITH ACORNS AND GUITAR 28

II.

COOKIES 33
WE WRITE WITH OUR BODIES 34
REPORT FROM THE PROVINCE OF HERON AND SWALLOWTAIL 35
IN THE DISTANCE LEARNING ROOM 36
LETTER FROM AN OHIO CLASSROOM 37
FIFTY BILLION PLANETS 39
BEST PRACTICES 41
ABANDONED HOMELAND OF EXILES 43
THAT THE GROTESQUE INHABITS THE MATERIAL WORLD 44
THE UNRELIABLE NARRATOR REPORTS ON THE NARRATIVE WORKSHOP 45
IN BOSTON 47
THREE FOR TRAKL 48
THE SORROW INDUCED BY AN INEXACT VOCABULARY 50
BLACK WATER SNAKE, COOL MORNING 51

III.

THE MAP OF MY SELF 55
FREE WILL IN THE LATE CAPITALIST ERA 56
QUASI-GHAZAL: ON EXPLANATION 57
KELLEYS ISLAND ELEGY WITH WIND AND HEARSAY 58
LISTENING FOR ORPHEUS 59
BEING THE SONG 60
SUBJUNCTIVE ON BURNTSIDE LAKE 61
AMBITIONS 62
IMPROVISATIONS AMONG THE LEDGES 63

The Mysteries in Yellow Springs 64
Natural Theology from the Sherman Bench 65
Meditation on Matter 66
Pavilion 67

IV.

Meditation on Narrative, Dogma, and Flight 71
Stringer 72
Brief History of Midwestern Civilization 73
Partial Catalog, April Sunday 74
Poem with Characters, or Cobwebs 75
Meditation with Good Posture and Swine Flu 76
Ohio, or Some Things Resisting Full Disclosure 77
Rhapsody in the Underdog Cafe 78
Further Notes on the Martyrs 79
March Ode on Beauty and Melancholy (Three Drafts) 80
The Eight Sounds 81
Some Intimations re the Elements 84
Something Is 85
Waterfall 86

Author Photo and Biographical Sketch 89

I.

THE BODY

and if we are not transformed, what is there to desire?
—John D. Caputo

Cool near the waterfall, creek louder than the highway.
Good in the dark, writing blind, everything close

and nothing clear. What else but to dream of another life
among such a roar, so much whelming water?

After dinner my friends talked of spiritual healing, of relief
from nagging pains and torments through a skillful touch,

manipulation of auras, so I told how my knee got sore
and swelled and clicked with every step for three days,

then slowly got better, all on its own. My story was
not well received, but I want to trust in mystery,

I wait each day for gifts I don't deserve, I am thankful
for lovely women who have healed me many times

without Reiki or acupuncture or even looking my way.
I believe in auras near and distant, and that our souls

are bigger than our bodies. My wife called in the middle
of this, believe it or not, to say she'd fallen off the ladder

cleaning windows and broken her arm. She's home,
not in danger but entirely annoyed, with a temporary cast,

a sling, and a prescription for Vicodin. *Don't worry,*
she said. I believe and trust she will be made whole,

but I doubt anyone will cure her at a distance. *There are
miracles,* says Caputo, *and there are cheap parlor tricks.*

The water roars. I'm almost ready to walk to the rail,
my eyes are getting used to the dark, I am reckless sometimes

but not stupid. The body is more than some clay jar
with a dismal eternal glob inserted. It is to be trusted,

especially when it says *Not too fast*. The waterfall twists
and rumbles, alien, unstoppable, coming up stunned

and foaming on the rocks, broken into froth and magic
every second, hurrying onward as if not changed at all.

What Do We Mean

—Underdog Cafe, Yellow Springs, Ohio, 7/12/12

My table is painted brown except for the shape that's flaked off,
like a biped lion, like a man with dreadlocks and a nine-mile stare.

My new friend says she has been photographed lying blindfolded
on a tile floor. I remember every face and not a single name,

so I keep smiling. And someone wrote *the words of the prophet
are written on the subway walls* on the wall of the local Subway.

And the girls walk by outside, semi-dressed for each other, and
the boys wilt like weeds in the damp heat. What if the prettiest girl,

silent all through lunch, should turn to me afterwards and ask
if it's all right for her to write song lyrics, *deep* song lyrics?

If no Christian rocker has either inspired or challenged my faith,
it's because the words "my faith" seem strange as "my river"

or "my universe." The guy in the corner is waving his pen, but not
my way. For three years I've managed to keep L. from enlisting me

in her crises. *Then,* she says, *it narrows down to strategic pillars.
I mean, again,* she says, *what do we mean?* What if this is where

the narrative arc tips suddenly, insanely, recklessly down
like the rockiest trail, the steepest slide in the waterpark?

What if I don't even remember the beginning, and suddenly
find myself in the burning ground, music flaming up

like red wings, like succulent and fatal crimson lips?

Many geese. Only one swan. And the windmill churning, churning
like a desperate signal, as if turning and getting somewhere

were the same, as if any mother's son could sit on a yellow canoe
and be at home in the world. And the turtles and muskrats

I will never see, the deer carcass I will not find at the edge
of the woods, the birds I can't name and their songs I can only

call lovely, shreds of the great song, real and passing,
warm and breathing, slender and spiky as the heron gliding

to the far shore. What am I missing? What did I know,
six or seven lives back? Does something still curl against

some wet spindle far inside, a shiver, an answer in a lost code,
a word like *crepuscular*, like *sister* or *thank you* or *yes?*

2.
The bat knows plenty about dusk, not much about us. The moon
and Venus are not looking down, though I am looking up.

The wide scud of cloud, like a first sweep of mortar for tile,
has gone gray already, the fire banked. Even the wind is resting

at last, and the blades of the windmill have stopped, off kilter,
like a child asleep on his feet. The birds want only to rest now,

and to wake with their mates beside them. The raccoon wants dinner
and a good muddy shore for washing. The moon would be a bowl,

if what I see could be trusted. If what I knew became solid, or true,
or even a dream in the mind of the world . . . If I were the mind

of the world, I would send the cars to bed with no supper, I would
skim like a flat rock into the sky, slip between the last cloud

and the last tree, circle and turn and fly unlaced and golden
into the dawn inside the dark. There's time for that and everything,

time to close the book and load the car, time to hurry north
and find our beds, soft and weary, lucky, lucky as we are.

SUMMER EARLY IN THE MILLENNIUM

To imagine you know is one thing, to know that you don't
is something else. My great-grandfather disappeared somewhere

between Alsace and Sacramento, turned up safe, never told
the story. Never mind emotion recollected in tranquility.

Think meditation in thunderstorm. And yet the intermediate
dog bane beetle remains, a living gem. The song sparrow's

regional dialects keep expanding. The chickadees will eat
from any patient hand. When my brother vaulted out the window,

a legion of snowy tree crickets bore him away. Or might have.
Amanda didn't tell us her birthday was in June, the same week

as the latest storm of the century, the same week I heard
the oily voices purr that all it meant was summer. It was

the year the self was demoted to mush, the year I dreamed
a row of eleven golden pies, the year Jann picked

two whole quarts of blackberries along Oak Hill Road.
Today I heard bird-sound, caught a dark shape swinging

across the path, heard the jumbled rush of notes again,
and thanks to Tom I knew it was the shy and lovely

indigo bunting. I went back to the room, the notes
of a new song forming in my head. I went winding up

stairways to a narrow room at the top. I met a carefree
Buddha and a worried Jesus. Any road gives two choices,

but when was that ever enough? Amanda got homesick
and left early. All I remember is her poem was lovely.

It's easy to take weather for climate, but thunder is still
thunder, wind is wind. The goldfinches bolted from the thistles,

but then one perched on the tallest stem, as if just for me.

CONTEMPLATION WITH OLD HONDA, CARNALITY, FISH

Who can go free to the God behind God?
—Fanny Howe

1.
I have no excuse, just some coffee. Everybody is sleeping in.
I do not have a huge deal for a book about punctuation,

or the crappy ancient Civic we all think M. should dump
as soon as she gets the first check. She agrees. *But if I get*

*a real ca*r, she says, *I'll have to find a garage to park it in.*
I have no more penmanship than ideas about how to find

the God behind God, but almost always I can read the scratches
I leave behind, and the pages somehow fill up. The day is gray

but dry. A low branch tips, sways, settles. *The wind is what*
I believe in, said F. *"God" is the failure of all the other words.*

2.
Say Jesus had a wife. Would it mean one more reinforcement
of heteronormativity, another wearisome oppression to bear?

A divine affirmation of carnality and delight, the Holy One
and his mate sweating joyfully, sweetly together? I know

almost nothing of Jesus except that he spent little time
comforting the comfortable, or afflicting the afflicted.

3.
For the third time I pick up the cup and find it empty.
There are voices from the kitchen, bread, jam, more coffee,

I only need to stir myself. *I was lucky to be poor,* said L.,
and lucky to escape it. I was lucky too, I never had to live

on squirrels and dandelion leaves, though one whole winter
I had just three shirts. I remember opening the dresser

each school day, choosing one, thinking it was simple this way.

4.
The fish like it under water. The river doesn't spend
its days saying "I am beautiful." Who needs things?

English was not my first language, but I remember
only scraps of the others. There are voices that carry,

voices that carry meaning. No voice for my yearning
for some final grandeur. The trees nod without joy or sorrow,

absorb all the light they can. It changes. It will change.

READING NEIL GAIMAN IN A WESTERN SUBURB

"This is a bad land for gods," said Shadow.
—Neil Gaiman, *American Gods*

The condo is small, neat, uncluttered. The streets
are quiet at night—the cops keep the hoodlums

away from the school. Between the trees and clouds
we rarely see the mountains, and these days Mum talks

only about food and relatives, and Dad can be amazed
by a row of cars, a long hallway, cherries. So I like

to sit in the floral chair that came from Grandma
and Grandpa and to slip off into magic and drama,

sex and murder. I like to roam the continent,
Kansas to Wisconsin to the House on the Rock

and Lookout Mountain. I'm happy no stray god
wants me for a bodyguard or a nine-day vigil

strung up in the world-tree Yggdrasil. I'm glad
someone is up to the task, if only in a book I read

in mechanical, ghostly memory, patterns fleeting
and unsteady as the hero whose name is Shadow.

Both the story and the telling trouble my mind,
but in that old, lovely way that even as a child

I yearned to be taken, to be troubled and amazed.
The best country for gods is the country of the mind,

the story, a country where shapes move over streets
and cities, highways and mountains, empty lots

and chain stores, move like an ancient crow or red-tail,
keen, hungry, and entirely without words.

CONTEMPLATION WITH DOORS, NESTS, AND MUSIC

1.
Unless I latch it, the bedroom door swings wide open.
The one at home swings shut unless we prop it with a chair.

There is no wisdom like the way things swing,
no mercy like the way dawn and dusk come calling us

over and over, the way a body demands to be filled
and emptied. Even today I think sometimes

that the world should pay attention, that my heart
and head ought to meet in the middle, that

the house sparrows should still be sleeping in the nest
with their latest brood. Tom told us last night:

the nest is more dangerous than anywhere else.
If somebody must get eaten, shouldn't somebody live?

2.
Does it matter which door we take? The cardinal sings
Rudy Rudy Rudy, Rita Rita Rita. The path makes

no complaints. I veer off from my last companion
and am alone among the trees. A deer runs ahead,

noisy, almost clumsy, leaving its sign in the wet path.
Deer trails thread off all ways, and I think

of the white footed mice sleeping in their burrows,
damp but content after the morning shower.

Cicadas in the red oak, dragonflies flirt and fight
above the pond, frogs twang their single notes,

and a line of people skirts the far rim. Their voices
drift back to me, scatter into the breeze and hush.

Would it matter if I gave up my job, found a little cabin
and lived for two years on rice and meal, ignored

my wife and children? Thoreau, Whitman, Dickinson—
bachelors all. I can barely remember being single.

The pond dreams of fire, and with every glance
of the sun, bits of its being leap free and spiral away.

3.
Outside the air is fresher, but every stranger
with an obligation is already growling up Everett Road,

rattling over the tracks, pushing the turns
a little too hard. I want food and coffee

and the last bagel with the last cheese and then
to sit with my new friends, to walk one more time

in the woods, to play my guitar while Bill
riffs around it on fiddle, flute, tin whistle,

while new hills and valleys spring up and fade,
new vistas and forests full of deer and wild turkey,

hemlocks and maple and beech and giant burdock,
bees and bats and earthworms and eagles,

all of it solid and breathing, steaming and singing.

Things I Didn't Learn from the Road

The trail curls around the cornfield and down to the towpath
just a few yards from the house. A fawn and doe clambering

away through the brush can sound thunderous.
The bees and twin butterflies love the noonday sun.

Despite what Rich said, I can walk Blue Hen to Buttermilk
in twenty minutes and not get either foot wet.

The trail and the musclewood trees don't remember me,
but my hands and feet remember them. The water's down

from last week's torrent to its usual midsummer trickle,
but still it sings and complains and pretends all this

has never happened before, every tiny step down
the long stair of the falls. Like Eternity and William Blake

I am in love with the productions of time. I know nothing
except to look and listen for the hot damp dry cool presence

of earth as it peers shyly from the edges of things,
whispers in crevices, floats and falls through fire and slate,

echoes in the weeds that cling to cliffs, roots that burst
dazed and disgruntled into sunlight years ago

and have been pondering their next move ever since.
There's nobody here but me and two waterbugs

who don't want to share anything, with me or each other.
Nobody here but the sleeping whitefoot mice and cicadas

and birds whose song is lost to me in falling water.
Nothing here but sunlight bent and laced and reborn

into 10,000 things, of which I have good clear names
for ten or twenty. Why am I so in love with water falling?

THREAD

if my life is a thread being pulled by a needle . . .

If the chimes of freedom flash like the flash that caught you
half a mile from home last night, still circling the quarry,

wondering suddenly where the ducks and geese find shelter . . .
All you knew was to keep going, let the needle in your head

pull you onward, sweaty and puffing again, lucky, keeping
the pace you can, almost too fast, hoping to get lost in the music

or your worries and forget for a while the labor and sweat
and small pains, heel, knee, ankle, the swing of arm, thud,

thud on pavement, just keep on, follow the pull toward
the next turn, the next familiar street, forget the thunder

or wait for it after the flash, feel the breeze and know the storm
will find you if it chooses, wind in your face or not, let it go,

the rain is cool and the shirt is wet already with your hot sweat,
too late to slow down, too soon to think of home, cross

the steel bridge and take the little rise up Spring Street, pass
the small familiar homes like a silent crowd, like people sleeping

in the pews, left on Elm to the Catholic church, good people
filing in to sing and pray but you must go on, right on Lawn,

you know what pulls you now, you know this last long street,
the time is good, the legs are weary but they bear you on,

your heart is firm and strong, the air sweeps in and out
of your open, deep, and secret lungs and somehow still

your blood takes what it needs and gives the rest away.

THE POET WATCHES HIS NEIGHBORHOOD

Those who didn't mow yesterday are mowing today.

A little of the corn is yellow and feeble from standing in water too
    long, but the rest is jungle-lush, eight feet tall, full of juice.

The neighbor's granddaughter has ridden her bike all day on a short
    loop that includes part of my driveway. She must be bored to
    tears.

This morning three girls walked by in tennis gear and the prettiest
    one kicked the junk paper somebody throws on the sidewalk
    every Monday. Every Tuesday I toss it into the recycle bin still
    in its plastic bag, though now I hear that the bags gum up
    recycling equipment.

It's another mild afternoon, inexplicable for August.

I don't have a gun or a cell phone or a sense of danger, but I suppose
    I'm on neighborhood watch.

I failed completely at protecting Trayvon Martin.

After the verdict, my friend scolded her white friends for expressing
    less Facebook outrage than her black friends.

Our new grandchild is pudgy and cute beyond belief, and won't let
    his parents sleep more than two hours straight.

I have been failing at outrage for forty years, riding my bike in wide
    circles on the square roads around my town, through the numb
    acres of corn and soybeans and wheat stubble, the rare
    woodlots, crossing the creeks which are full of muddy water
    this year.

I wear my helmet and my biking shorts and my moisture-wicking
    shirt, I look in my little mirror for cars roaring up from behind.
    I check my speed and mileage on the quarter-sized device I got
    online for ten bucks, keep the time on my watch.

For an old guy I'm pretty fast: ten miles today in 33 minutes.

Not much wind, a good bike, no traffic to speak of. I got home sweaty
    and satisfied, needing to start dinner.

At the swinging bridge I took a break, but the mosquitos drove me
away.

Two dogs at one place, but they didn't try to cross the big ditch. An
old steel windmill, torn down except for the bottom eight feet
of the frame.

A billboard near the interstate, facing away from the county road.

Then I sat on the screen porch with a glass of cold water and a towel.
The neighbor girl was still doing laps on her bike. She only
glanced at me when I tried to say hello.

Two long-haired kids on skateboards rattled by, and a girl with her
little brother. Some SUVs and little Hondas.

Quarter to six. Turkey brats for the grill, fresh sweet corn, squash,
tomatoes from the garden. Trayvon is still dead, his killer still
free. Most nights we remember to lock our doors.

All the ground is still standing, with no help from me.

APRIL WITH GARDEN AND GUILT

My garden's going nowhere. Too much business, school business,
poetry business, driving for hours to read a few poems

and drink temperately with friendly near-strangers who
hand me their cards in the vain hope I might find them work.

Weak ties are crucial, I heard last week, and I believe it.
Think of Gulliver, pinned down by a hundred threads.

A hundred little worries and promises in my inbox.
My garden, still slimy with the hard winter and the rains,

still cold but thawing, warming, the little seeds of crabgrass
and morning glory and stray tomato almost ready to wake.

I could hire my neighbor to till it—he's been on disability
since Vietnam, but he punched a college kid whose girlfriend

peed in his bushes on her drunken way home, and since then
I've hesitated to ask him. His cats and dogs are sleek and plenty.

Twenty bucks, maybe thirty, and he does a fine job. Last year
I spaded up the garden myself, poorly, and can't say why exactly

except his number isn't in the book, I have to open his gate
and walk up and knock on his door, go past his signs in praise

of shotguns and dogs. I've never owned a shotgun or a dog.
His wife delivers mail. His kids were in school with my kids.

He lives six houses down. When I dropped by to pay him,
we'd talk a little about the weather, the soil. I wanted

to let him know I hated the war but not soldiers, not him,
but where to start? Except for his dogs and his signs

and his skillful hand with a rototiller I have no idea
what his life has been, what he was doing while I filled out

my CO papers and went off to college, how dark his days
or bright his nights, what jungles he's still slogging through.

WHY I GET THROUGH MOST DAYS IN PROSE

Should there be poetry for the leak dribbling onto the hardwood below
the stairs, softening plaster, peeling paint?

For the tree full of bird-noise on Spring Street, shrieks and whistles,
glides and tweets, yet even with binoculars I could only find five
starlings nestled calm on a high branch?

For the brown water pressing north in the Little Riley, the squawking
ducks almost hidden in the weeds?

For twelve vultures in the high dead branches, fourteen more on the ridge
of Centennial Hall, spreading their dark wings to dry, gliding
back and forth like old men changing tables at the diner?

For these new black hikers that don't hurt a bit right out of the box and
don't leak like the last pair did?

For the Gaisberg and the Untersberg, cobbled streets and church towers,
voices speaking German, Czech, Korean, menus in four languages,
fortress frowning over it all like an old man who's forgotten what
he ordered and isn't pleased by the look of his plate?

Yes, all of that is far away, except in my head. Still.

For 14 pens 2 pencils a yellow highlighter and a blue sharpie tilted every
which way on my desk, along with nine scraps of paper with
unread notes to my future self.

For the desktop holding them all plus telephone, stapler, computer,
scattered folders and the latest *APR* and *Seed Catalogue* and *The
Way It Is*, *Poetry in America* and the *PMLA* I'll send over to the
library unread again, *Down in My Heart* and *Primitive Mentor* and
Naked Poetry (why did I dig that out?), *Approaches to Literature*
and the Special Georgian Issue of *International Poetry Review*.

For the people sparking in my head, Joel in his bare room waiting till we
can haul his stuff across the border, sad Lisa with her inscrutable
updates and her dozens of bad poems by heart, smart Lewis and
nine more from the workshop in the woods, Karen whose whole
kitchen got trashed when a water line blew with them out of
town, my dad whose shoulder won't stop aching, these are the
lucky ones, so many more, what comfort will we find in poems?

SAFETY

I've lived my life in safe places, not at risk except for boredom and its associated disorders. The farm was safe, my room upstairs with my brother, the pale kitchen where we ate, maple cupboards my dad built and the plastic table we inherited and still fold our clothes on today. I have no tales of terror at home, no drunken parents, a bully or two but not such big deals really.

The dangers were from beyond, the ones that scared me: the Russians, the fallout from our own tests though we heard nothing about that until much later. God leaning down to decide whether I was worth saving.

Under the hot comforters my mother had stitched, below the leaky upstairs windows, I felt entirely safe from what I could see and exposed to everything I couldn't. The Russians were crazy, they didn't care if they died, they didn't want supermarkets or Jesus, all they wanted was to rule the planet whether it glowed like charcoal or not. And Jesus would never want anybody like me, willful and impolite to his teachers, sullen and recalcitrant in his secret heart, unable to resist saying the wrong thing too loud at the wrong time.

The stairs were gray painted wood, two of them broken a little and tilted enough that if you hit either one wrong in socks you'd slip and bang, bang, bang all the way down to the bottom and not much to console you there except Mom saying what, you fell down *again?*

Sniffle and suck it up, go back upstairs, through my sisters' room and into the spare room that was mostly empty except for my worldly uncle's trunk, which had nothing I was interested in but a heavy, hard, beautiful M-1 rifle pilfered from his time in Korea. It seemed absolutely perfect in its every curve of wood and steel, its mechanisms and rods and staffs, even its silence and refusal to do anything but shift in small ways and click gently, casually, confidently if cocked properly and its trigger pulled. It lacked only an agenda, a round, something to send off like a small, clear message to whomever it might concern.

What did I dream as I handled the weapon, lifted it to my shoulder, sighted down the barrel? I had fired guns, my own BB gun and the .22 my dad had for skunks. We were pacifists, the church taught, but nobody worried about plinking at cans and birds. These were the days when every third man was a veteran and the Good War was still fresh, and I had seen plenty of battles on TV. We played Swamp Fox and cowboys and Indians in the tall grass behind the house, arguing over who was dead and who wasn't.

Still, all I can bring back about the rifle is its feel in my hands, its weight and size and simple, ruthless, solid economy. Sooner or later it disappeared, but I don't remember that either, or much else about the world in those days beyond the open acres we farmed, the quiet fields and the noisy tractors, school and church and the books I lost myself in whenever I could. I don't even remember when I first discovered that even those distances were only the most partial, fragile, temporary shelter.

PRINTS

Any list I can make will be a joke. Woodpecker, though, mosquitos,
    violets and columbine blooming, the idling creek.

Halfway across the swinging bridge, I slow to let it settle.

Nurse log, home to mosses and a few thin weeds, a family of those
    brilliant tiny round red bugs, a black spider that ran straight at
    me when I spooked it.

The way the far bank shoulders up, allowing the roots purchase and the
    trunks to poke upward.

All this instead of rock and methane frozen into durable mush, instead
    of hard vacuum, neutrinos, enormous furnaces.

Not instead: in addition.

The tentative way of the black and orange butterfly, inches from my
    sweaty knee.

So many bodies, the wet god whispers, *so much to love, to fear, to lose.*

I am a disturbance here, but not an absence.

If I want I can sing as loud as any cardinal.

I always start out too fast and too loud.

A raccoon's been down at the shoreline, left its infant traces behind.

Not much changes. Everything moves.

Late sun on the warm creek-skin: a soft jewel, never to be mined.

ODE WITH WINTER SUNSHINE, ONE MIND, FOUR HOUSES

The winter birds, pleased by the sun.
Snow pushed off some of the sidewalks,

packed flat and slick on the rest,
minor ruts and chunks on the side streets.

The big red house, the little white house,
the yellow brick house and the red brick house

all seem delighted to have made it this far,
mainly intact, furnaces roaring quietly

in their cellars, shingles locked
in place, doors mostly latched.

The houses might be saying
We have ridden out another night,

and that seems strange and hopeful
when once again the streets are

passable if not clear, the walks
are passable if not clear, and a little man

in a long blue coat wanders by,
a little late as always, snug in his jeans

and boots and sweater, his mind
passable, passable if not clear.

Contemplation with Acorns and Guitar

Night gathers in the pines, but the grassy slopes aren't ready
to give up. The fireflies and the frogs have things to do.

I have a good post to lean on, a stolen pen, lots of paper.
Tomorrow we'll explain, apologize, surrender. Tomorrow

the heat will return, and fat men will tell expensive lies to make
themselves richer. Tomorrow more cattails will die,

more glaciers will calve, acorns will fall from the trees.
The rhythm of the world has nothing to do with saints,

everything to do with bodies. Even on a single path
there are always more than two ways. One law is waiting.

One law is doing something, right now. Maybe it's opening
your eyes, after all these years. Maybe standing up, or sitting

in the packed privacy of the trees, in the places between,
places where things breathe on their way to the sky.

When we start back the air fills with something not fog,
not dust, filmy, almost light, all real, the secret net

of the world shaken out just for us. Let it all stay soft,
let it linger and shimmer around us. Let it all stay.

The page almost glows in the last light, it crazes and
glitters, reads itself without me, it soaks in my words

and gives back something else. Even the birds know better
than to speak this late. It's not dark. It's only less brilliant

than it was. Remember that kid you called dumb? We are
all asleep in the outward man. We are all deaf in the world

of light. Even in the darkness it's hard to hear what
we need. There are words to love: *willow, bullfrog,*

mud. Things that lie waiting for centuries, like a fiddle
forgotten in an attic, barely breathing in the heat,

the dark. It isn't lost. What's a century or two?
Not every tree has a guitar in it. But some of them do.

II.

COOKIES

—after Neruda

I'm tired of being respectable. And professional.
For too long I've gone into classrooms and bathrooms
and churches, smiling and brittle as a garden gnome,
or a homecoming queen waving to the cold bystanders.

The aura of solid houses makes my insides quiver.
I want to walk into every one—houses I've passed by
for twenty years and never entered.
I want to sit in the big recliners, steal cookies
from the jars on kitchen counters, riffle through magazines,
check in medicine cabinets and under beds
for scandalous revelations.

I'm tired of being available. And polite.
I'm ready to be invisible, grouchy, and stupid.
I'm ready to stand up in the middle of the meeting
and scratch myself on the way out the door.
I'm ready to bring my guitar to class, set up between
the students and the door, play every song
I've ever played, every song I can remember,
without explanation or apology, whether or not
I remember the chords or can hit the high notes.
"Louie, Louie." "Kumbaya." All nine verses
of "Stuck inside of Mobile with the Memphis Blues Again."

I'm ready to be a bad wizard, to change morons
into moonshine, dutiful drudges into parsley,
solid citizens into Corvettes and cottonmouths.
I'm ready to fill up with gas on the way out of town
and stick to the township roads, so narrow
that somebody has to take the shoulder.
To drive a wide spiral until I find God
or Lake Erie or the providential,
proverbial, preverbal Mississippi,
so low now I can barrel right across it
with barely a splash or a slither and sail on
into the blue-gold American night.

WE WRITE WITH OUR BODIES

Among the choice of useless things, which do we give our minds to?
—Valéry

The bodies around the table can't imagine not talking,
and even though I hush them I agree. Their every word

is lovely and necessary, no matter how dumb and desperate.
I don't know them and will never see most of them

again in this life, but we manage an agreeable circle.
They answer my questions, they argue and laugh,

and even the spectacular red-haired girl
and the smart dour guy at the end of the table

seem un-cruel and almost pleasant, not the kind
to drive more than one or two kids to tears or worse.

So when we've had our laughs and I've tried
to fit "spontaneous overflow of powerful feeling"

and "small machine made of words" together for them,
and they've moaned and grumbled with the strain

of thinking outside their tender young beings,
they ask for paper and bend over it as if they believed

they could write their way out of anything,
they scrawl and scratch, the chairs tink and clink

as they shift. And the soft murmur of pens is like
bees in the pear tree, like water over stones,

like wine poured in a goblet, poured out free
and dark and precious. Take it, take and drink.

REPORT FROM THE PROVINCE OF HERON AND SWALLOWTAIL

1.
We are finding small bones, cupping tiny shrew skulls
in our palms, squinting at their elegant planes and absences,

their vivid red teeth. Bergamot and salvia, Virginia creeper
and tupelo, gray and red dogwood, wild apple, tree cricket.

We are hearing birds we cannot see, chipping sparrow,
vireo, peewee. The ponds are low but the frogs and goldenleg

spiders still thrum and weave, the heavy cattails bend
and tip back up. We still have water for drinking and washing,

and since the first night the food has been bountiful. Alone
I'm no good at seeing things, but the widow skimmers

are hard to miss, chasing and posing above the lily pads.
A tiger swallowtail sways on the teasel, trying every gap.

2.
The green heron came to fish in the sewage pond, but
settled grumpily in a tree. The common yellowthroat,

skulking masked warbler, does not want to be seen.
The moon gets fuller as it rises. Yes, it's good to talk,

good to shut up and let the bullfrogs take over. Let us
learn to live swaying. Let us curl inward, like snakes.

Forget the names of the birds, the songs we never learned.
Make the shrill whine of cicadas into lemonade, penicillin,

centuries of bliss. Tonight our little tribe has everything
we need. Young and old, straight and bent, inked and plain,

tonight none of us will search our pockets for a dollar,
or suck off a stranger for money, or shoot up anything

but moonlight. Some pond creatures will eat, some get eaten,
mosquitos will labor off full of our blood, but tonight

every mother's son and daughter will sleep dry and cool.

IN THE DISTANCE LEARNING ROOM

All these faces, lit from inside: the red-faced man with cane,
the wheelchair woman, the reporter, the young mother, her little

blond girl who's coloring in the wash of our talk. The scientists say
you can't really do two things at once, but years ago in church

my boys rattled their trucks along the pew, asked later
if the preacher really saw a ghost come down the stairs.

I don't remember where I need to be next. I don't know
why I can't stop coughing, I don't know if I can twist the lid

from this evil water bottle or why they made me take it.
I may never know whose shoes I was meant to fill,

or who saw my shoes and knew I'd abandoned style for comfort.
I know the sky is up, and east and west don't require windows,

which is good since there are no windows. When I asked
for comments the whole set of strangers settled in their seats

and then invented the poem all over again in a rush, from
the coat tree to the heart transplant. I could barely keep up,

so I just kept nodding and pointing at the next person and saying
yes, yes! I was told that from the distance learning room

everything can be transmitted anywhere, at the speed of time.
I wanted to send our talk everywhere but instead I asked them

to write and the room hushed. The girl with the crayons
leaned into her mother, who wrote anyway with her free hand.

We read to each other as the time allowed, and at the end
we clapped and smiled. A few stayed after, spoke of friends

in common, thanked me. I thanked them, forgot their names.
Everything we say exists forever, I believe, but only

the atoms will remember, and words are not their thing.

LETTER FROM AN OHIO CLASSROOM

Such an attitude stems from a tragic misconception of time,
from the strangely rational notion that there is something in the
very flow of time that will inevitably cure all ills.
—Martin Luther King, Jr.

I'll let you be in my dream if I can be in your dream.
—Bob Dylan

The theme for the day is not dream but time, time in its magisterial
indifference, sacred or profane only as we make it, shape it,

as we read its scars, its tracks, its dreamy traces. *How is it*
with the nothing? Heidegger asked. *Where shall we seek*

the nothing? We may not comprehend the ensemble of beings,
he said, *but we find ourselves in the midst of beings all the same.*

He wasn't in my dream as we talked about injustice anywhere,
direct action, creative tension. I imagined shutting down

the government out of fear that poor people would get health care
and so destroy the country. I said nothing about that.

One guy complained that he couldn't bring his deer rifle
on campus. *Prejudiced against rednecks,* I heard him mutter,

and found myself suggesting that he just keep it in his trunk.
A guy in the first row shook his head. Somebody read the part

about getting all the facts before taking action. When I asked
for an example and the guy in the first row said "Girls,"

a stir ran around the room, but then we shrugged and smiled.
We'd all been there, we admitted, blacks and whites, guys

and dolls. Some of us lived in the midst of beings we could
not comprehend. One of us hated her stepfather even more

than her brother did, but kept up a mask of mere hostility,
seething, sullen, lest she be thought lacking in respect.

We all knew time would not cure our ills. We all wanted
to be in somebody's dream. We all had trunks full of guns

and time and being, full of nothing, nothing to hide.

FIFTY BILLION PLANETS

The galaxy is crawling with life. What's for dinner?
—Anonymous

Hemingway was wrong about the very rich, and when he walked
into my nonfiction class I told him so. He wanted to punch me,

but I told him all physical violence on campus was prohibited
by the Peaceful Menno Code, so he just glared and stomped

out the door. The Code also prohibits gloating, so I asked
the students what we'd learned. "You blew our chance to talk

to a famous dead guy," said the smart kid. "And a rich one," said
Melinda, who never said anything. "Yeah, but rich people *aren't*

like you and me," I answered, weakly. "You mean they don't
attach lame adverbs to their speech tags?" said the smart kid.

I opened my mouth to tell him off graciously, within the guidelines
of the P. M. C., but just then the door opened and a sweet voice

said, "Qu'ils mangent de la brioche." I was baffled, but the Code
requires unconditional intercultural affirmation, so I smiled

and nodded. The woman sashayed towards me, glittering
as she walked. Fifty billion earthlike planets in the galaxy

and there she was, a golden, liquid comet on a collision course
with my poor sinful earth. She circled me, twice, and then she

was more like a hawk pondering whether it was worth the effort
to swoop down and snatch a meadow vole. The students

were spellbound, Hemingway forgotten. "Everyone thinks
you said, 'Let them eat cake,'" I muttered. "Everyone in your

stupid country, maybe," she answered. "As if the whole world
speaks your silly language." She slid a finger from my ear

to my chin, and I shivered, but then she turned to the class,
and she was not at all a vain, dead queen. "There are

fifty billion earthlike planets in the Milky Way," she said. "How will you spend your small, strange, unrepeatable life?"

BEST PRACTICES

I don't know how I accomplish anything. Mostly I think
it's frantic bursts of half-conscious & desperate action
fueled by aggravation and the desire to get back to the couch

and sit on my butt. Mostly my days pass getting ready for things
or getting over them, plotting intricate optimistic stratagems
and then grieving their dismal collapse, the befuddled silence

that follows my best questions, the awful pauses that persist
despite all my strategizing, desperate improvising, and bull-
headed confrontations. And now we are engaged in a great struggle

to do everything better, to discern and designate and inculcate
best practices in every crack and crevice of our days and nights.
No student will ever be bored. Every single one will embrace

the system with grand delight, rush to the library for six books
and read all night. Their thirst to know will blossom until
even the keggers and raves will be full of passionate conversations

on Foucault versus Freire, solar versus wind versus geothermal,
the discourse of white privilege as yet another overdetermined
iteration of white privilege. Every notion, every thought

and dream, will be linked to tangible social outcomes.
The gardens will bloom right through the winter, tomatoes
gleam scarlet in the snow, the beefy linemen will insist

very gently that the cheerleaders discuss their deep feelings
and views on childrearing over tea. When I walk into the room
the students will have filled the board with questions,

they'll be grilling each other on Whitman's view of the body
and the soul, flinging lines they've memorized back
and forth like shuttlecocks, like birds that spring to life

and spiral around the fluorescent lights, larks and crows,
exultant and murderous, here a flight of wrens, there a heron
stony and severe as death himself. And the foolish and the strong

will be full of love for each other, and the raped and abused
will shine and smile suddenly, and the brilliant will be quiet
until they are needed most, and the crazy, the wild

and the bitter will speak the words that will heal us all.

ABANDONED HOMELAND OF EXILES

How else to describe this absurd, lovely world? And yet
the trees stir themselves into the humid air, take the weather

as it comes. Maybe it'll kill them, but not today. Praise
for the mutilated planet is insufficient but essential.

I'm all in favor of grief, mercy, and language, but what kind
of meal do they make? Whose children will they save

from minimum wage or the poverty draft? Still, it's the season
when despite all my moans and whines the rooms fill up

with strange and lovely faces and we revel in the happy
weariness of learning names, explaining badly, bearing

our loads of ill-defined matter and impractical passions
like sticks and tinder for the illegal fire we hope to burn

when we find that lost hollow, the clearing with three rows
of skinned logs for seating, fire ring, blackened kettle.

Yes, the trail's overgrown, root-rough, yes there might
be snakes, yes mosquitos for sure. Wear jeans and socks.

Bring the guitars, the song sheets. Uncle Jim will say
something genial, solid, and a little awkward. We'll sing

and sway, praise each other and walk back in the dark,
holding hands. Then we'll gather what we need and head

off again, for good. The exit doors will open if we push
and wait and push again. Let the alarm bells blaze.

They'll stop us. But they'll have to let us go.

THAT THE GROTESQUE INHABITS THE MATERIAL WORLD
(with apologies to Michael Moore)

> *Our ability to perceive images as grotesque may be the*
> *emblem of original sin, marking our once and future intimacy*
> *with the divine.*
> —Geoffrey Harpham, *On the Grotesque*

The rabbit lady's house is white and cold. The rabbits don't mind,
nestled in their tawny fur. She holds them as you hold a child

to be admired by a stranger. She has no child, only a bastard ex
who pissed away both their wages and then the plant closed down.

The rabbits are better company. Erhard Schön made Martin Luther's
nose a pipe played by the devil, who rides the rebel preacher

like a monkey, blowing heresies into his ear. Luther seems
bewildered but not frightened, still alert and almost calm,

nearly ready to rail against the peasants and the Anabaptists.
Straining for sublimity in bed, we ape the beasts. Which of

the seven deadly sins is the most grotesque? *I might be a serial killer*,
Misha admits, to nervous chuckles. Bram Stoker spent four years

composing his first spellbound letter to Walt Whitman.
There was that lot of him, and all so juicy. Does animal cruelty

always lead to worse? Who does not love and fear the shock
of broken borders, the monstrous hybrid. The revelation

of the tender skin laid open, the shocking, pragmatic organs.
The terrible knitting of human and beast, the paralysis

of the gaze and the tongue. I had lunch once with the director
of the Institute for Bodily Transformation. She was writing

proposals, assigning reviews to the postdocs and grad students.
The book is all here, she told me, pointing to her right ear.

I muttered something about Kafka and Borges, and she said
her funding had been generous. The rabbit lady rubs a docile buck

under the chin, asks her customer *Do you want them for pets or meat?*

The room is full of people thinking hard about premises and
what-ifs, story arcs and shadow arcs and three-part structures.

The mushy middle is so hard. Suppose several billion people
and uncountable other beings are in this big pot, and most

of them just want love and something to eat and drink,
and one guy is sitting in the top row of a chilly auditorium

scrawling on his yellow pad and the others are calling out
answers: *Dorothy! The Witch! The ruby slippers!* What does

the wizard want, anyway? One can be the antagonist
without being evil. The baby screeches like a banshee, but

in two minutes the maid calms her down. Despite the wizard,
Dorothy can go home as soon as she learns to tap three times.

Never mind the silly speech about finding it under your feet.
I don't want to talk about it anywhere, Jack said. *My favorite villains*

are the heroes of their own story, said someone down front. *The key
to narrative is leaving almost everything out,* I said to myself.

2.
Hannibal Lector didn't want to be evil, just . . . well, what?
Nobody seemed ready to explain that one. End each chapter

a little early, said the expert, keep them turning the pages.
Usually by page 60 I've used up all my ideas, and then

it gets tough. The main character must be transformed.
Or the reader. Or the Shire. You don't need to drop

a dead body on page 1. They're drinking sweet tea,
but the murder photos are in the briefcase. A narrator

with Asperger's may be viewed as unreliable. Avoid head-
hopping, unless you really know what you're doing.

Consider the blind man's point of view. Consider

"Bob was turning green" vs. "Bob was going to throw up"

vs. "Bob threw the pistol into the river." How well
do we know good old Bob, really, after all these years?

In Boston

I spent three days in Boston and never got more
than four blocks from the hotel. I walked for miles

on concrete and tile and marble and industrial carpet,
trying to memorize the routes and failing, wondering

over and over if I'd passed this store before, this huddle
of chairs and tables, this heap of Russian dolls or beads

or covers for electronic devices. I passed a thousand
people and another thousand, fast and slow, plain and

beautiful, rich and poor and indeterminate, locals and
tourists and visiting poets like me with giveaway lanyards

and name tags, shabby clothes and sore feet. I said
sorry a hundred times and received it that many more,

all of us in a hurry but polite, steering clear whenever
we could, bearing our bodies through the crowds

like a batch of silent marbles thrown down a long chute,
looking and not looking, sneakily studying each face

that approached just in case it might be the one,
the friend I'd not yet seen, the long-lost teacher still

alive and strangely ageless, the gray-eyed woman
who was surely not put on earth by God to please me,

who never glanced at me, but blessed me in passing
anyway. On Boylston the bars were full,

but we found a table to lean on and eventually
some stools. We drank two beers each among the kids,

who were loud, flirty, drunk enough to seem happy.
Slush was melting along the streets. Nobody said

the second bomb will go off just outside, but not tonight.

THREE FOR TRAKL

1.
Like the burrowing of a field mouse or a mole,
the woman searching her gray bag for the slippers

she left beside the bed. Like searching Trakl
for a line without desolation and beauty:

rotten branches, holy brother, gentle lyre-play.
Now the left-handed women are quiet,

writing carefully in their small notebooks,
recording the three important dreams they dreamt

while rain spattered and trembled in the downspouts.
Madness, lonely, dying. Ruin, darkness, stars.

2.
Against all logic, Trakl is unusually translatable.
He was crazed in that peculiar modern way:

aware that disaster was bearing down, escape
was impossible, beauty and God as useless

as trenches and machine guns. Red wine,
ether, veronal: precious and insufficient.

Her face is floating through the waters.
Her hair is waving in bare branches.

What garden, what sister, what mountain
could deflect or distract him? *Like a wound*

her mouth is open. His life a limping journey
toward one doorway, a vast room heaped

with the stinks and groans of empire burst and blown
through the flesh of farmers and schoolboys.

Heal us, they surely begged, help us. He had
some rags, his hands, water. He knew the doses

and protocols for opium, ether, he could see
the neat rows of bottles on shelves in Vienna,

far away, so clear. He had nothing, some odd lines
from his own poems, fragments of Grete's piano

echoing in the lost upstairs rooms in Salzburg.

3.
Almost impossible to sit still. Chilly rain, October,
the furnace balky in this borrowed house. We huddle

at the stove, put on our jackets, make futile phone calls.
All over Salzburg bronze plaques on walls hold

Trakl's poems up to the rain, the sunshine,
the Föhn wind that still kicks up in autumn,

bearing dust and melancholy. We are in no danger,
but we talk of failed systems, bitter nights

and blunders, leaks and disasters. The empire
creaks and groans, pumps straining at nothing,

brown bitter fluids spilling from the pipes.

[Passages in italics are from *The Poems of Georg Trakl*,
tr. Margitt Lehbert, 2007.]

The Sorrow Induced by an Inexact Vocabulary

Dostoyevsky insisted that his late hosannah
had gone through a great furnace of doubt. I was deep

into college when I managed to learn the concentration
required to spell those Russian names. By then

my eyes were already weak, yet with my $600 glasses
I can still read easily that human eyes were sharpened

by millennia of watching for snakes. Yes, the world
remains full of barely visible dangers. Yes, Sinatra's

blondes were preened and polished, languid and silent,
yes, it was music to make love by, no, we do not know

whether he or his blondes suffered the sorrow induced
by an inexact vocabulary. Yes, the philosopher Geber

compared the incredulous to children shut up in
a narrow room, who deny that the great world exists

because they have no window to observe it.
Yes, Caputo said that God settles into the lowest

pockets, the recesses formed by the little ones.
Yes, we have much testimony, yes, and plentiful

evidence, and yes, we ought to know by now.

Black Water Snake, Cool Morning

Today the bands of muscle answer slowly,
the long spine creaks. At the pond edge
the duckweed thins and the greenish hoppers

wait sometimes, but this is warming time,
slow lift of the head out of water, above the log,
tipping back, tipping, curve and press, push forward,

dark log and the water releasing, colder still at first
in the plain air as the skin dries and then begins
to gather the weak sun, the dark skin,

any thought but to stretch and lie still
is the wrong thought, any day with log and
even weak sun is a good day, flick of tongue,

yes, eyes open eyes close, yes, the snake dreaming
is not other than the snake awake except
that time turns buttery and vague,

duckweed stipples the long body,
the slow breath and flickering signals.
No need to eat yet. No need to ponder or hope.

The cosmos wheels, gods and empires spiral,
blaze, wink out, a child points and whispers,
the snake's dark length absorbs it all,

a black mirror open to the sky, a boundary
between art and truth, fact and paradise,
song and water, sympathy and time.

III.

THE MAP OF MY SELF

1.
I was seven then. Teachers kept insisting
that I shake all my stuff into a flat bowl

before we started, that I had six minutes
to draw a map of myself. *The opposite*

of guilt is clarity, said Cory, and that
seemed a comfort. What is the opposite

of guitar? *Freeway*, I said. *Penmanship*
matters. I'm so glad you're here.

2.
The path to Furnace Run, dusty, hot,
the creek mostly dry. Even my new camera

can't make the parched weeds shine.
Document or invent? Pay attention

or just make stuff up? A few rusty pebbles,
a spray of leaves lit by the sun,

already turning bronze. One brief,
tiny opening is all the camera needs,

all it can stand. Without the guitar
I'd have lost myself long ago. I still

don't have a map. I hate freeways,
but they brought me to the woods.

Free Will in the Late Capitalist Era

The long slow mills have no choice, the freeway has no choice.
The empty fields have no choice, when the snow falls they agree

to turn white and later muddy, when the sun burns they parch
and crack, learn to be tough. What choice do I have, wakened

at dawn, bleary and empty, except to stand up and totter on,
slowly gather the pieces of myself, the day ahead ordinary

or not, who will arrive and who depart, on the radio a new
calamity far away. Eat something, drink something, pull on

my shoes and coat and walk through the back yard of the brick
house whose owners moved out months ago, the knobby grass

soggy from the last rains, smelly gifts from the neighbors' dogs
hiding in the hollows. I have no choice and I'm one of the lucky

ones, one of the last ones. Who else will have such an easy
sweet time of it, tucked into this town like a child into bed,

free to leave any time I can afford it? What else can I do
but slide my card in the slot, pull open the door, trudge

up the stairs to the desk where the whole day is waiting?

QUASI-GHAZAL: ON EXPLANATION

I hate explanations. My own are generally full of rationalizing,
Guilt, and evasion. No, I love explanations, especially my own.

No. So many words. I can't believe they keep coming to me.
Soon my quota will be gone, and I will just wave, point, and grunt.

No. I love every word, so lucid, so plump, so worthy.
Redolent as the manure spreader kicking in to spread sheer bullshit.

The world is a grand heap of extravagant and odorous claims.
What can we do but offer even more extravagant bullshit?

Think of the writers we love best, Whitman, Blake, that poser Emerson,
His handyman Thoreau—every one a grand, proud bullshitter.

Maybe not Dickinson. Mary Oliver? Is it just the men?
But think of *Wuthering Heights*: every page, transcendent bullshit.

And Keats. The saddest, loveliest bullshit. "I shut her wild wild eyes
With kisses four." The cold hill side. Explaining. No birds sing.

Kelleys Island Elegy with Wind and Hearsay

This deafening dirty roar was the wind's idea,
but the water agrees over and over, then says *wait*

when it's far too late, the sand already all up
in its skirts. The trees nod but they're troubled,

they almost remember the last time this happened.
The gulls skate sideways, sure that something

interesting will turn up. For once the breakwater
is earning its keep. And yet a hundred yards inland

it's all hearsay and innuendo, rumors the low weeds
toss off without a thought. One more scandal,

one more line buzzing in a starlet who forgot
her panties on purpose, what's it to them?

At the boardwalk's end a soggy trail, and a sudden
white tail. A flight of cormorants surfs the torrent

on their way south, hoping this is lucky as it seems.
On the alvar shore it's easy to believe the waves

are pouring down a long slow hill, they bruise
and bounce so angry, so off-kilter, in such a hurry

and then so lost about their next move.

LISTENING FOR ORPHEUS

O you lost God! You neverending trace!
Only because hatred tore and scattered you
are we hearers now and a mouth for nature.
—Rilke, *Sonnets to Orpheus* 26

This room with unplayable piano and diabolical fold-out sofa,
this room with awful wallpaper and fine ornate molding.

Room in the middle of an island quiet as underground,
quiet as space in the last hour before sleep.

Room full of vanished strays and sleepers, absent outsiders,
sad aunts and gay uncles, traces in the corners, skin-flecks

under the table, under the sofa of ghosts who slipped away
intact and happy enough to have escaped the maenads,

to have been neither torn nor scattered, neither lost
nor divine. To elude the furies should be blessing enough.

To sleep in a room where even the sound of the rain
reaches only your dreams. To dream a dark street

shining beneath the old and erotic trees, to dream
a music born of wood and air, fire and muscle, leaping

and astonished, three voices none of them your own.

BEING THE SONG

And I still don't know if I am a falcon,
or a storm, or a great song.
                    —Rilke

So I could be a song. But a great song? Or a bluegrass tune
with a decent chorus and a shift to the minor to savor every time,

and a break I can almost play. Or one of those wordy obscure
Dylan tunes that nobody remembers except the fanatics,

one he's half-forgotten himself, or drags out at the end
of the concert and screws up totally just to be contrary.

Or one of those earnest dull protest songs everybody my age
half-knows, played by the equally earnest guy whose heart

is in the right place, who can almost hit the chords and the notes
and will repeat the chorus at the end to make sure you get it.

Or not a song at all, but an answer to a question nobody asked.
Light from a hidden source, so the room seems dark

but the page is bright. Or a window filled with knotted wood
and greens, the shape of someone barely visible as they pass.

Subjunctive on Burntside Lake

If you close your eyes and lie under the sky, tiny creatures
will begin to explore under your clothes. And if you lie still

they will guide and direct you, they will show you pageants
and signs in the clouds, sheep that safely graze, concubines

and cuckolds taking blissful, nearly just revenge in each other's
arms. And your way across the water will be clear, and the boat

that carries you swift and quiet, and the oarsman will steer
easily over the deep water and between the lovely islands,

through the channel to the far shore. And when at last
you offer the coin, he will turn it back to you, and touch

you gently with his strong hand, and ask only for your name.

AMBITIONS

These are woods that forgive everything but forget nothing.
—Tomas Tranströmer

To be a forest dense and green enough to hide a million creatures

To be the vine grown right to the top of the tallest tree

To be the man whose job is to save the tree by sawing through the
vine three feet up

To be the bench waiting just when a man needs a rest

To be the sign that answers the question the man hasn't asked yet

To carry back the names: willow, buttonbush, boxelder maple,
spatterdock and fragrant waterlily

Water smartweed and the endangered wapato, midge and mayfly and
whirligig beetle

Green darner dragonfly, vivid dancer damselfly

And always the large dim roar of many narrow waves hurrying in

To stand at the edge until one laps at my shoes

To touch the water and think *I could swim*

To cross back over the barrier beach, the only human sound my
footsteps

Many insects, a high gentle wind stirring everything

Countless volunteers, the last sign remembers

To volunteer at last

IMPROVISATIONS AMONG THE LEDGES

I guess the ledges are here so the children can yell and scamper, so they can read the carved names and tease, Josh, why'd you carve your name?

I guess it's because the birds need territory and competition to make them sing.

I guess God got tired of stones and silence and decided to try something else.

The hemlock curves like a drain pipe into the rock, it's never had enough water or soil, it's skinny and lopsided, almost feathery. But here it is.

Can the other girls persuade the timid one to jump the crevice? Should they?

The sun is having another good day, ducking into niches and tiny plains, improvising more brilliant geometries.

The wind and trees have worked up yet another set of untitled variations.

Anything with feathers or fur has settled in for a nice siesta.

Unlike most places in America, if you don't climb on the rocks or steal firewood you have a legal right to be here.

Time passes quickly here, the paper falls to the leaves and rots away, the great slabs of shale and conglomerate slump and melt like butter in the heat, the old world dissolves and the next begins and the man in the blue hat still gazes up into the ledge, gestures to his friend, puzzled, his camera battery dead and the girlish voices drifting down, buttery with giggles and trepidation, trying to convince Amanda to leap from one world to the next.

THE MYSTERIES IN YELLOW SPRINGS

"Rat!" he found breath to whisper, shaking. "Are you afraid?"
Afraid?" murmured the Rat, his eyes shining with unutterable
love. "Afraid! Of Him? O, never, never! And yet—and yet—O,
Mole, I am afraid!"
> —Kenneth Grahame,
> "The Piper at the Gates of Dawn,"
> *The Wind in the Willows*

The buskers on Xenia Ave. had a new song:
At least it's not as hot as yesterday! It was still hot

but the spring was still cold, the girl dumped her water bottle
to fill it with the iron-dense water. *I don't like it*

but I want it, she explained to grandma. Baby sister
reached toward the shiny stream, looked back at Mom

to be sure it was OK. The water kept saying something
small but insistent to the rocks. Susan told me that the rocks

were all set in place not long ago, that there's a buried
tank, that the handy strand everybody drinks from

was designed that way. Well, that's helpful, I wanted
to tell her. It's hard to tell if the rocks agree or are grateful

for the company or are bored to tears. They are orange
from the iron, not blushing or confused. Like the girl

with half her head shaved, they don't care who looks.
They might be the shelving steps nearby, the ones

nobody notices and everybody walks on. They might be
buried anywhere, with worms and moles for company.

They might be here when the Piper steps out at last,
goat-footed and dappled, shining like sun through

new leaves, too strange and grand to look in the face.

Natural Theology from the Sherman Bench

—East Lansing, May 2003

If I really loved Jesus I would surely not be here in the sunshine.
I'd be trying to love the poets now reading in a room without me.
If I really, really loved I would not even think what I think

and it would go easier. Because my neighbors' dogs bark
at dawn for sheer joy. Because like them I have known joy.
I have matched and folded the family socks, survived history

so far, seen my small desires satisfied. Did I come all this way
to sit on a bench? Did the ragged goose feather once have a home?
It's too hot to sit long in the sun. *Can we, can we, can we,* the girl

asks her mother, and her brother hitches his pants and runs fast
as he can down the wrong path. His sister calls and he runs back,
sniffs a yellow tulip. *Oh do what you want* says her mother

and the new weeds, and the cardinal says *I will do what I can.*

MEDITATION ON MATTER

Doesn't it matter that you have existed all of your life?

All my life I've been matter. Big news, right? This coffee,
still too hot to drink. The music—tuneful disruption

of the ether, lyric, maybe apocryphal, not at all apocalyptic.
Sticky pine cone, snake-tangle of cords, paperbacks titled

American Earth, Derrida and Negative Theology, and *My Brother
Is Getting Arrested Again:* matter, matter, matter. It all

matters, or so I must believe. But how to reckon, sort,
articulate? When I say *None of this is true,* mark A or B.

When I say *Ready, steady,* get in your stance, but don't
jump the gun. Who can say this matters, this does not,

yellow buses wait for their children and the sun has broken
loose again and liquid guitar runs shiver and vanish

like wind in poplars, sun on the skitter pond, swifts banking
and swooping through their high neighborhoods, all this

matter and all so luscious, heaped and sorted and tinkered
into shape and form and sound, boys and girls on the sidewalk

with bookbags and trumpets, school over and the cookie jar full.

PAVILION

empty cathedral, where . . . the memory of an
unknown home comes back to me.
—Rubem Alves,
The Poet, the Warrior, the Prophet

Last night my roommate snored, loud,
like a chain saw starting up and cutting out,

just enough silence to make each new
snort a fresh shock. I got up after

twenty minutes, found a couch, lay there
for an angry hour, stubbing my toes

on the short arm, missing my wife's soft
murmur beside me. I know I'm lucky,

this is nothing, but I thought I'd never sleep.
I stewed and brooded, turned, and finally

saw a great pavilion, green and yellow rafters,
many paths and corridors. *Go in* I thought

but could not right away, *go in*, and it
changed, became a cathedral of sorts,

and then something like a great open
forest, or a hall—others wandered there,

quiet, holding nothing in their hands
but other hands. And then I went in.

IV.

MEDITATION ON NARRATIVE, DOGMA, AND FLIGHT

> *It is still beautiful to hear the heart beat*
> *but often the shadow seems more real than the body.*
> —Tomas Tranströmer

My people are not natural storytellers.

Ask my father for a story, he's still trying to get it going
when all the boys have drifted off to the kitchen.

Still, I want the reader as far inside of my skin as possible,
no matter the difficulties. For instance:

The self does not feel like matter, but that's all it is.
I forget who said so, and I don't agree,

but it was spoken with such confidence.

And so much else needs to be considered:

Kites make the wind visible.
Some tree frogs can only sing for three nights.

Can you tell me how it is that light comes into the soul?

(That was Thoreau, 1851.)

Spirit is to religion as love is to marriage.

How do you run faster? Start running faster.

How does the box kite manage to fly?

"This is wonderful" and "this must continue" are close kin.

And then the kite's shadow across the plowed earth.

STRINGER

We were all asleep in America in 1970 when some farmer
near Minonk needed a pole barn, and so we'd pile

into Jerome's pickup and drive out breathing his awful cigars
and trying not to think how hot it would be by noon.

A pole barn is money stretched and pounded thin,
a wide high space closed in fast and cheap as possible.

As it goes up everything is high and shaky. I don't mind heights
if I can plant both feet on something solid. There's nothing solid

on a half-built pole barn. My palms are sweaty just putting
this down. I was the young guy and so I clambered up and out,

sat on one 2 x 4 stringer 12 feet up and took the next one
Edwin poked up and wrangled it in place and nailed it fast

and clambered even higher. My whole body insisted this
was crazy. Deep breaths and calm thoughts were useless.

By noon I'd burned a week's adrenalin, just not quite panicking.
Coming down was incredible, like escaping the sabertooth,

being pulled out of traffic. Two weeks and it was done.
Two fifty an hour, college money, money to work with my feet

on the ground, with my palms dry, money to live in a big old house
and choose my neighbors. Maybe I am still asleep in America,

maybe somebody is gaining. Somebody is ready to climb out
on any truss or stringer for a few bucks. I would do it myself

even now if I had to, if I was told to, if it was part of the work.

BRIEF HISTORY OF MIDWESTERN CIVILIZATION

Grandpa's Ford panel truck was powder blue
and held exactly six chicken coops, the wooden

kind that would hold fifteen or twenty
near-grown pullets, or the cardboard boxes

full of yellow chicks. We could get many more
in our red F-150, but if it rained they got wet.

Grandpa knew everything about chickens
and a whole lot about everything else, how

to buy ice cream, how to let me adjust
the heat in his car, also a Ford. He knew

how to do everything but keep his heart
beating, or what to do about the mess

in Ukraine, the oligarchs looting everything,
Putin riding smarmily along the border,

burning tires in Maidan and the hasty
barricades somehow proof against

the beetle-shelled riot police, the snipers
sent in from the north. And because

or in spite of all this the fields behind
our house sprawled out for miles,

peaceful as cows even when we got rid
of the cows, the fields bare and gray

in winter, the snow scoured off by wind,
the fences yanked up, the fence rows

piled and burned. Then spring, the corn
implanted and the black fields flushed

with ammonia, lush in August
as a jungle that only knows one word.

PARTIAL CATALOG, APRIL SUNDAY

Forsythia yellower than a crayon, daffodil and cherry blossom, corkscrew
willow fraying green along every seam.

I rode four miles and nothing hurts. I learned about plans for Tuesday at
11 all next year. I was given some numbers and told to call.

Instead I copied some poems about writing poems for Annie and Lowell,
who are writing poems.

K. walked up the driveway and crossed the street, her blond hair
swinging like the flag of a secret new country.

A man came by wanting to give me a free written estimate.

Our three battered trash cans are upside down at the curb, like hovels for
the three unholy fools.

Nobody's home but me.

One warped board on the porch ceiling gapes into a space nobody's
visited in sixty years, and a girl with a plump dog jogs by, and a
young man in a cherry-red car, and *you heard me* yells a father
down the street, not quite angry yet.

Nobody's home, I almost wrote.

Out on the roads, my children steer toward home in their battered cars.
The basketball they left on the porch at Easter is still rolling
around.

I should bring in the trash cans, dip myself some soup.

The catalog will never be finished, and what could be better?

The universe is mostly cold and empty.

Across the street the young mother sent her daughter in to practice,
checked her hair in the rear-view mirror, turned on the radio and
settled back.

And the April rain still finds its way all down and around us all.

Poem with Characters, or Cobwebs

Yes, Ricky was an Oklahoma hick. But Sandy,
Sandy could become inordinately aroused
at the mere sight of a respectable citizen
or a train robber. But then, somehow
in high school I got herded into going out
with Peggy, though I found her neither attractive
nor interesting. I found many girls both
attractive and interesting, so this was
frustrating. Later she may have been
abducted by aliens, or married twice
and had three kids, or become a man.
I never heard. But experts agree on
the importance of going through the motions,
so we danced in somebody's dark basement.
It was mainly just hugging and swaying,
so at least we succeeded at that part.
Her eyes were green, maybe, but most
of her was white as milk or snow, and not
much firmer. Neatly made though it was,
the bed in the corner of the basement still
looked like an unlucky cake. We did not
check under it for cobwebs. If Peggy was
inordinately aroused, she never let on.
And sure, she was a little heavy, but she
deserved better from me, from that dark room
where we were too young and baffled
to do more than sway and sweat. We only
had 45's, and somebody had to pick
a new song every three minutes, "To Sir
with Love" or "Ruby Tuesday." When
you change. Still I'm gonna miss you.
Mercy mercy. There's a kind of hush. Mercy.

MEDITATION WITH GOOD POSTURE AND SWINE FLU

Were we ever among the chosen? Did we seize on this place
too late, or too soon? Is all this temperate sunshine

a blessing or a threat? We all say aye when prompted, then
we mostly say nothing for a while except for the speaker,

then we say aye again. Somewhere sailboats are gleaming
in a harbor, especially beautiful if somebody else

is paying the marina fees. *We hope things are going well,*
says the speaker, *if I had me a shotgun, I'd blow you*

straight to hell. No, no, that's just a song. I haven't thought
about blowing anyone to hell or anywhere else all day,

though I own lots of stuff that could be lethal in the right hands.
But the real question is whether we agreed to agree, or not.

Some of us find it natural to scowl at students who chat,
doze, or text when we expect good posture and deportment.

I thought I heard my name, but it was just my first name.
Beyond borders, said my friend Paul, we hope for conversation,

contentious and otherwise. If I were Phil, I'd call myself
Phill too. The auditors have arrived by bus, Jim says,

but will leave by sunset. Eric didn't bring his swine flu file
but will talk for a while anyway. Go home until

the fever breaks. Cough into your arm. Use the hand sanitizer.
The shots will be free, which means somebody will pay.

OHIO, OR SOME THINGS RESISTING FULL DISCLOSURE

Do you have any idea how exotic this place is, my friend from California demanded.

I suppose I do, I answered in the Ohio fashion, meaning Tell me more, meaning Convince me, meaning Not much surprises us.

She just kept looking and talking, the chain link fence along the bike path, the teddy bear store on Main Street with 2 x 10's bracing its walls— the snow broke a roof beam, though we think it can be fixed.

The back yards all garden and grass, too hot or cold to inhabit most of the year.

The gray cat on the sidewalk just off the state route, splayed in one last, almost graceful plea. It'll be gone tomorrow, I said, as if that helped.

Vegetation without irrigation, streets empty in the middle of the week, and clouds so bored they wait around for days, just in case.

Cold yellow sun through black branches.

Girl running, one arm swinging loose, toward the door and her warm room.

Two toy collies in a backyard on Bentley Avenue, one barking at me and at the other one.

We looked at a house when we moved to town, long ago. Two women were living there, with two collies, and they told us they were moving to a house on Bentley. We haven't seen them since.

The six red cabbages my neighbors planted, then ignored.

The big fleshy leaves lay flat against the dirt through weeks of drought.

When it rained at last, somehow they lifted up, and even grew a little.

Their heads like purple baseballs, stunted and alive in the first snow.

New ice lacing the creek stones, a map of delicate elevations and relations.

Twenty-five years in the same house.

New collies.

RHAPSODY IN THE UNDERDOG CAFE

The word I forgot was language. The language I remembered
was enough, I guess, at least no one left the room, or threw me out.

Run your fingers through my soul, reads the poster, but I don't
believe I will. We're barely even friends. A happy 3-piece band

is playing in a corner of the Underdog Cafe. My new friends
didn't know any of their songs, but I knew them all—"Wagon

Wheel," "San Francisco Bay Blues," "I Can See Clearly Now."
The second cup of coffee is a dime cheaper and better

than the first. Next is "Seven Bridges Road." I want to be here
and at the Yellow Spring both at once and that's all right,

I'm almost there just thinking about it. *There is the taste
of time sweetened honey . . .* Wherever we are,

the world is with us, in us, tunes and words and ghosts,
bridges and rivers and roads. I've played so many songs

for myself, filling in the missing parts in my head, but to have
all the voices, to have an oak table and four swallows

of warm coffee left, is good. To have two more hours
and the whole Glen to wander is better. I don't need

to play chess or say a word, to write every day or wear
my good pants because it's Sunday. I can dwell

in the cloudy sweet piano chords as long as they last, until
the coffee's gone, until I remember the word for words.

Further Notes on the Martyrs

Our speaker has a tongue screw with him, though
it is a replica. He speaks of spectacle, witness,

dying well. One group's criminals . . . Stories
are not preserved by accident. Heroes are made

necessary by the nature of memory. Life is stronger
than death, and that is why we must praise.

I think. Identity depends on memory,
which depends. You might get in the book

if you merely suffered. We strive to maintain
an empathetic view of the oppressors, but we believe

that truth is real and can be known and practiced.
Therefore we praise the martyrs and the beauty

of holiness, even the beauty of rose windows
and artful representations of the Cross.

When the grieving villagers sing "Holy, Holy, Holy"
over the mass grave, surely this is beautiful,

though we cannot clearly say why. We cannot
believe that death is the mother of beauty,

the lovely wound that sends the child in search
of poetry. Surely we shall know the truth,

now and in the place of fire, on the pages
of fire, in the voices and bodies on fire, in the ashes

where the child bends for the tongue screw,
in the moment when he grasps the iron,

still warm, and straightens to show his brother.

MARCH ODE ON BEAUTY AND MELANCHOLY (THREE DRAFTS)

1.

But the most familiar and usual cause of love is that which comes by sight,
which conveys those admirable rays of beauty and pleasing graces to the heart.
—Richard Burton, *Anatomy of Melancholy*

March has been wind and sleet, gray and chill,
a last thin shield of ice on the ash stump,
a mat of maple spinners waiting to root
and sprout, dog dung, doves and sparrows
and one shy flicker fleeing as I shut the door.

2.

The eyes as two sluices let in the influences of that divine, powerful, soul-
ravishing, and captivating beauty, which, as one saith, "is sharper than any
dart or needle . . ."

I trudge the damp grass, cross the street, looking for a thrill,
a dart or needle to sting me awake. I've been burning
through paper clips, generating hundreds of unbillable hours,
filling envelopes with bad news and hasty critiques,
scrawling plaintive queries and complaints. *Miniatures*
are big around here, someone says, and we all nod. *Poetry books*
kind of freak me out. We scribble on the good poems and bad ones,
sail them across the big table like messages without bottles.

3.

Give me but a little leave, and I will set before your eyes in brief a stupend,
vast, infinite ocean of incredible madness and folly . . . who can sufficiently
commend or set out this beauty which appears in us?

What is it I want? I have love and money, a warm bed,
books and songs in piles around me, friends, wine, guitars,
a grandchild on the way. What heart was ever satisfied?
What I want is nameless, it lives in books, paintings,
the stories of lovers who will break everything for a day,
an hour, who rub and touch and sing as though they can
turn each other into flame, break into blossom, spin
so fast they rise and fall at once, become both dark
and light, split and fuse, surrender and triumph,
kneel and stand, leap and shout and moan and lie down
happy, sad, full and empty, finally at ease.

THE EIGHT SOUNDS

1.
A heavy door with a round metal seal attached, me on the other side
in the easy dark. I drove a few hours, took a room in another house,

took a few steps out. Left and right, two frogs—not contending,
just singing, and women laughing & cleaning in the kitchen.

There are eight sounds, the monks told us last week. They are hard
to name in your language, but they include frogs, wind, hands clapping.

If I could learn to paint with sand, tip it carefully through the bronze
cones bit by bit, I'd be thankful, but would I be happier, or closer

to abandoning desire? After the monks spoke I went home, tuned up
the 12-string and played "Water of Love" twice. It felt so good I did

"Peggy-O" and "Satisfied Mind" to boot. Nobody heard me, and
I put the guitar away and made supper, but maybe you can catch

an echo, deep in the ground, carry that water of love to you.

2.
"Seven Bridges Road" and "She Loves You" revolve in my head
as I walk the quarry floor—jumbled stone, straggly firs, rubble.

Interior music is one sound, a well of nervous joy, enemy
of contemplation. I slept well in a bumpy sort of way, kept waking

to find that the arm I wasn't sleeping on had lost all feeling. Fallen
asleep, we say—a phrase both true and wrong. Like an old quarry

with a shallow new lake at one end. Like a monkey mind chattering
and romping among the wrecked rocks, catching on wind in leaves,

traffic, crows, startling, gaping, losing itself moment by moment.

3.
I believe in the good life, or at least my right to name its attributes:
today it starts with open water and sunshine, with petroleum

and late capitalism. The goldenrod sways with the butterfly's landing.
A small plane flies right overhead. In my dream the border agent

was grilling my Canadian wife: did you even *get* a degree?
what have you made of your life? The fourth sound means one thing

but holds something else, as when X said *Steak and eggs, please* and meant
Only those who take Jesus as their personal savior, as when Y says *Of   course*

I understand instead of *Eternity is not long enough for you to suffer.*

4.
The fifth sound is the monks rubbing the ridges of one sand cone
with another, sending a thin stream of color from the fine tip

to the surface. They lean close. *I am allowed to do the grass, which is green
and smooth*, explains the monk with good English: *it is easiest, but still*

very difficult. The largest sand mandala took 26 days to make. It was
swept up quickly: impermanence is essential. There is a photo, which

the monk with good English shows us, but it is impermanent too.

5.
The sixth and seventh sounds, I think, can only be explained
in a lost Tibetan dialect, and the eighth has never been named,

though the monks have argued it for years in the courtyard,
staying up past two though they must rise at five for prayers.

6.
The monk said: twenty years sleeping, twenty years working,
ten cooking and eating, five in the car, and your life is gone.

He didn't even mention football, surfing the web, changing oil,
or making love. He didn't mention walking the North Shore Trail

alone, contemplating Lake Erie from a solitary rock, waves thumping
gently. The black arrow of a cormorant, two feet above the water.

In the mornings we study and memorize, said the monk,
in the afternoon we read and argue. Maybe in twenty years

we are ready to teach. Another cormorant still faster, still lower.

7.
The small waves murmur against the rocks. They have been
arguing almost forever, and love the quarrel more than anything.

I have excellent boots and a fair sense of balance. I intend
to return and tell the tale. I mean to keep God out of it.

The little islands hold up their trees and houses,
all together in the sunshine. Everything I need for now

fits in my pockets, and my hands are still free.

8.
All eight sounds carry near the earth. The last sound
carries everywhere. The seagulls rest on the waves,

fly when they please. Above, a great stretch of sky,
a scrim of cloud, then not much for a very long way.

SOME INTIMATIONS RE THE ELEMENTS

1.
Fire is helpless without air.

2.
Air is in love with fire, sometimes happily.

3.
Fire requires earth, is everywhere in earth,
returns from earth,
but fire loves only itself.

4.
Water will sleep with anybody,
has no morals and no ideas,
no program except to argue
with earth about where things
ought to be, and how big.

5.
Sometimes water will dally and talk
for hours, if the rocks are sharp and shapely.
But what water really loves is sand.

6.
Wood is in love with water and with air,
with earth and with fire,
but they pay no mind to wood,

they make love inside the cool leaves
and the hot leaves, sparking and arcing
of atoms and tiny strings,
lovely surging noise we have no ears to hear,
air and water, earth and fire.

7.
But wood can hear, wood listens
and grieves and says nothing
and lives, lives swaying
to the beautiful noise.

SOMETHING IS

The wood smoke smells so good it's like a meal.
The beach open and empty, a few gulls bobbing,

one fisherman. Wavelets ripple in with their small news:
the world still awash with inscrutable information.

Half-heard voices from under the rainfly, three young men
at ease between breakfast and lunch, clink of the campstove,

Yeah, good idea. Ow, Lord! Scuffed tracks in the sand.
Horsefly shares the bench with me, just a moment.

A. said she wrote about goddesses for years, and never
even noticed. *Really,* she says, *I recognized myself*

just last Saturday for the first time. The alphabet
took us into the rigid plain of our left brains,

like a thousand-acre cornfield, and we've been
stuck in the flats among the monochromes and

right angles, people of the line and the book.
The world has only one page. It is not best read

left to right, top to bottom. It has many seams and edges,
places where secrets and treasures may be found if one

walks slowly, alone or with a lover or your dogs
whose names are Norman and Under. *We all make*

something out of nothing, said G.C., a true believer.
Unlike him I'm full of earnest doubt, and sure I can

make nothing except out of something, especially
when I cannot say just what that something is.

WATERFALL

So I didn't get the instructions. So the pond's full
of grainy duckweed, bumblebees in damp clover,

dragonflies and damselflies, twittery birds. Young Will
keeps saying things like "This could be lava!" Two hawks

swoop and soar. I think they might see paradise
just over the brow of the hill, and because I'm not

Kafka if I could climb those skies myself the mighty
keeper at the gate would usher me in graciously, show me

to the holy sun porch where God and I would sit, drink
coffee and compare our griefs, our big defeats and

little victories. And the sweet air will zephyr all round us,
carrying birdsong and creek babble, and we will agree

that things are dismal but not unusual, and that a certain
cockeyed hope is still required of us. We'll walk a long way

through the beeches and tulip poplars, and at the waterfall
we will peel our clothes and splash in the shallows,

as close as we dare to the roar and rush, and its every
syllable will come clear suddenly. And then everyone

will be there, your friends and mine, our enemies too,
all the strangers holy and unholy, and in the water's spell

we will touch our perfect bodies and our minds and
remember everything. And we will laugh and dance

and make meta- and physical love until the very universe
shivers and glows. And when at last we are healed, sated,

complete, we will lie down in the long meadow grass,
the dragonflies basking and soaring all round, and sleep

in the roar and the silence for as long as our dreams require.

Acknowledgments Continued

I'm extremely grateful for the many friends and fellow travelers, widely scattered but essential, who offered advice, good company, love and edification as these poems came into being. Thanks to the Quarry Hollow writing group, and Susan Carpenter for bringing me into it; my many friends, colleagues, and supportive administrators at Bluffton University; the Cuyahoga Valley National Park co-conspirators and students, especially Terry Hermsen and Bill Walker; Ann Hostetler for inviting me to teach a short course with some brilliant students at Goshen College; and my long-time poet friends Jean Janzen, Julia Spicher Kasdorf, Clint McCown, and Keith Ratzlaff. Thanks also to my wife Marlyce, our multi-talented sons Nate, Ben, and Joel, and their spectacular partners Jessica, Jennifer, and Martha. And thanks to twenty, fifty, a thousand more good and golden people living and dead, trying to see that it all goes on.

ABOUT THE AUTHOR

Jeff Gundy, long-time professor of English at Bluffton University, has published six earlier books of poems and four of prose, most recently *Somewhere Near Defiance* (Anhinga, 2014), *Songs from an Empty Cage: Poetry, Mystery, Anabaptism, and Peace* (Cascadia, 2013), and *Spoken Among the Trees* (Akron, 2008). His earlier Bottom Dog books include *Rhapsody with Dark Matter* (2000) and *Inquiries* (1992). A 2008 Fulbright Lecturer at the University of Salzburg, he taught at LCC International University in Klaipeda, Lithuania in spring 2015. He plays 6- and 12-string guitar, and puts in as many miles as possible on his road bike and (with his wife Marlyce) on their Cannondale tandem.

His poems and essays have appeared in *Georgia Review, The Sun, Image, Kenyon Review, Christian Century, Mennonite Quarterly Review, Conrad Grebel Review, Nimrod,* and many other magazines Other honors and awards include multiple Ohio Arts Council fellowships, two C. Henry Smith Peace Lectureships, Bechtel and Yoder Lectureships, a Nancy Dasher Award, a Society of Midland Authors Poetry Award, and the 2015 Simons Lectures at Bethel (KS) College.

Jeff is the winner of the 2015 Ohio Poet of the Year award from the Ohio Poetry Association.

Recent Books by Bottom Dog Press

Books in the Harmony Series
Stolen Child: A Novel
By Suzanne Kelly, 338 pgs. $18
The Canary : A Novel
By Michael Loyd Gray, 196 pgs. $18
On the Flyleaf: Poems
By Herbert Woodward Martin, 106 pgs. $16
The Harmonist at Nightfall: Poems of Indiana
By Shari Wagner, 114 pgs. $16
Painting Bridges: A Novel
By Patricia Averbach, 234 pgs. $18
Ariadne & Other Poems
By Ingrid Swanberg, 120 pgs. $16
The Search for the Reason Why: New and Selected Poems
By Tom Kryss, 192 pgs. $16
Kenneth Patchen: Rebel Poet in America
By Larry Smith, Revised 2nd Edition, 326 pgs. Cloth $28
Selected Correspondence of Kenneth Patchen,
Edited with introduction by Allen Frost, Paper $18/ Cloth $28
Awash with Roses: Collected Love Poems of Kenneth Patchen
Eds. Laura Smith and Larry Smith
With introduction by Larry Smith, 200 pgs. $16

* * * *

Harmony Collections and Anthologies
d.a.levy and the mimeograph revolution
Eds. Ingrid Swanberg and Larry Smith, 276 pgs. $20
Come Together: Imagine Peace
Eds. Ann Smith, Larry Smith, Philip Metres, 204 pgs. $16
Evensong: Contemporary American Poets on Spirituality
Eds. Gerry LaFemina and Chad Prevost, 240 pgs. $16
America Zen: A Gathering of Poets
Eds. Ray McNiece and Larry Smith, 224 pgs. $16
Family Matters: Poems of Our Families
Eds. Ann Smith and Larry Smith, 232 pgs. $16

Bottom Dog Press, Inc.
PO Box 425/ Huron, Ohio 44839
Order Online at:
http://smithdocs.net

RECENT BOOKS BY BOTTOM DOG PRESS

Sky Under the Roof: Poems By Hilda Downer, 126 pgs. $16.
Breathing the West: Great Basin Poems
By Liane Ellison Norman, 80 pgs. $16
Smoke: Poems By Jeanne Bryner, 96 pgs. $16
Maggot : A Novel By Robert Flanagan, 262 pgs. $18
Broken Collar: A Novel By Ron Mitchell, 234 pgs. $18
American Poet: A Novel By Jeff Vande Zande, 200 pgs. $18
The Pattern Maker's Daughter: Poems
By Sandee Gertz Umbach, 90 pgs $16
The Way-Back Room: Memoir of a Detroit Childhood
By Mary Minock, 216 pgs. $18
The Free Farm: A Novel By Larry Smith, 306 pgs. $18
Sinners of Sanction County: Stories
By Charles Dodd White, 160 pgs. $17
Learning How: Stories, Yarns & Tales
By Richard Hague, 216 pgs. $18
Strangers in America: A Novel
By Erika Meyers, 140 pgs. $16
Riders on the Storm: A Novel
By Susan Streeter Carpenter, 404 pgs. $18
The Long River Home: A Novel
By Larry Smith, 230 pgs. Paper $16/ Cloth $22
Landscape with Fragmented Figures: A Novel
By Jeff Vande Zande, 232 pgs. $16
The Big Book of Daniel: Collected Poems
By Daniel Thompson, 340 pgs. Paper $18/ Cloth $22;
Reply to an Eviction Notice: Poems
By Robert Flanagan, 100 pgs. $15
An Unmistakable Shade of Red & The Obama Chronicles
By Mary E. Weems, 80 pgs. $15
Our Way of Life: Poems By Ray McNiece, 128 pgs. $15

Bottom Dog Press, Inc.
PO Box 425/ Huron, Ohio 44839
Order Online at:
http://smithdocs.net

www.ingramcontent.com/pod-product-compliance
Lightning Source LLC
Chambersburg PA
CBHW031146090426
42738CB00008B/1240